Reclaiming We

Reclaiming We

Reclaiming WE

Twenty Everyday Acts to
Strengthen the Common Good
and Defend Democracy

From **CIVIC NEBRASKA**

Edited by Steve Smith

CONTENTS

Part Three: Choose Empowerment

Part Four: Choose Optimism

Introduction

HOW DO WE STRENGTHEN OUR DEMOCRACY? It's a daunting question for most Americans, many of whom have spent more time than they would care to admit consuming articles, surveys, and commentary in recent years about how the United States is in danger of backsliding into an illiberal pseudo-republic or, even worse, autocratic rule. Compounding the worry is that the question just seems to, well, persist without a clear answer. That is, we Americans don't want our democracy to become weaker; that much is obvious. But we're unsure what concrete steps we, as everyday people, can take to do anything about it.

There's voting, of course. And that noble act is something millions upon millions of Americans do when called upon. In the 2020 general election, voter participation skyrocketed to levels our nation hasn't seen in more than a century. That our democratic systems functioned so well during an uncontrolled pandemic is notable, and it is worth celebrating, even though at historical highs, our turnout rates still lag behind other established democracies.

But democracy doesn't begin or end at the ballot box. When we use the term *democracy*, we mean more than just our system of government. At Civic Nebraska, we define democracy as a practice, a way of life springing from devotion to the common good. In this sense, a modern and robust democracy requires more than citizens following politics closely or speaking out for our chosen candidates. Democracy is much more than the procedures, institutions, and norms that make up our governmental system. And it extends beyond the act of electing leaders and then leaving it to them to fix things. It's not a top-down deal: Democracy lives in the consistent and persistent actions of everyday Americans. It's in all of us. In our words, in our deeds, in our civic actions, and in how we interact in our free society with the good-faith goal of keeping it accessible to everyone.

It's almost cliche these days to say that we're at a crossroads; the fact is, no matter the era or the circumstances, when you zoom in closely, we almost always are. As co-creators of our interconnected, interdependent, shared democratic reality, each and every action we take matters to the whole. As the saying goes: *You're not stuck in traffic, you are traffic.*

Civic Nebraska created this book as a reminder of the power each of us possesses. To reinforce that all of our actions, whether big or small, official or unofficial, or inside or outside established power structures, compound. And to help answer the persistent question about how we strengthen our democracy. One fork in the road—ethnocentric, exclusionary—is familiar; the other is expansive and inclusionary, and worth fighting for. We can either devolve further into the recent pattern of apathy, cynicism, and pain, or we can pursue a much different path, one that ensures a powerful democratic future for ourselves and future generations.

The task before us is difficult and complex. Just as democracies can advance, they can also retreat and fall into peril if they are neglected and mistreated. They require their people to take responsibility for the well-being of one another, and therefore, their democracy, and also to innovate in how we address modern challenges to it.

The good news is this: As individuals, we are far more powerful than we give ourselves credit for. Collectively, there's no limit to what an engaged, informed, active American people can do. This short edition connects us to the fundamental ideals that have bound our country together for nearly 250 years: representative self-government that protects and enhances our equality, as well as our rights.

Taken separately, the 20 actions that follow may seem simple when considering the challenges of our time. But together, they highlight a mighty civic fabric that has stood the test of time. This guidebook can be used to activate citizen muscles that may have gone dormant, and can be passed along to friends, neighbors, and loved ones so they can flex theirs. It can help leverage the recent surges in engagement and activism into lasting democratic power. It can help build connection and community so that the coming challenges can be addressed collectively. And it's a reminder that we must *all* do our part to advance a democratic society that values respect, learning, and responsibility.

There's no time to waste. Let's get started.

PART ONE

Choose Community

We're better when we work together. A community thrives when people trust each other and show up for one another.

1

Reclaim *We*

Americans don't have to agree on everything.
But we must start from a place of understanding
that we are all co-creators of our interconnected,
interdependent, networked reality.

IT'S A CLASSIC LESSON. At some point in our schooling, usually in eighth-grade civics and then again in twelfth-grade American government, we are introduced to the idea of *we* and how, collectively, *we* make up our democracy. We're the authority. We're the last word. Embedded in our founding creed is the noble idea that democracy is based on active citizenship and civic duty.

We the people. *We* hold these truths to be self-evident. When we show up, lead by example, hold themselves and others accountable, and put trust in our fellow citizens, we all are better off.

Does it feel like that to you today? No? Maybe? Sometimes?

Once, unity was the most important aspect of our identity. The American *we* comes from the original state of joining as a whole to confront a shared challenge. The idea of *we* is important in our national narrative, that mythical self-definition that affirms and reinforces our national character and values.

To find their myths, other countries tend to rely upon their shared ethnicity, culture, or language. The United States, though, could not. In 1776, we lacked a single ethnicity, culture, and language. Our American experiment first emerged because of an argument, during a Revolutionary summer, under the banner of a radical idea that all people were created equal. The United States came to be as a mutual aid, which was officialized in a resolution addressed to the British Empire.

But this vaunted unity didn't happen automatically. Before the Founders actually put ink to paper in the Declaration of Independence that they were "United," they had to take one of the biggest leaps of faith in history: Trust in *one another*. This wasn't a slam dunk. The Continental Congress was often so unwieldy, so heated and divided, more than a few colonies threatened to walk away at times. But eventually, the men in that hall came to realize that their very presence together in Philadelphia meant that they were already acting as a nation, and that a problem for one was a problem for all. This truth was self-evident—as was the fact that they were responsible for one another, and for all Americans. They forged the very first definition of the American *we*, ending the Declaration by famously pledging to each other their lives, their fortunes, and their sacred honor.

That's how we've liked to define ourselves. When we're at our best, that's the American *we*. In the centuries since, we've obviously made advances: What started out as a coastal confederacy run by white male land- and slave owners is now a pluralistic, multi-ethnic democratic republic that spans the continent, with a modern focus on expanding individual freedoms. This is something that's never been attempted in the history of the world. This is worthy of applause!

Or, maybe not, if you look around a bit. Today, that original American notion of *we* has become quite frayed. Today, there's a lot of "otherizing" in America. We see it in little ways, in how we live, where we shop, what media we consume. We see it more significant ways, too—in persistent racial violence. We see it in increasingly wild cycles of economic booms and busts that seem to only solidify the haves and the have-nots. We see it in ever-escalating political turmoil and crisis and brinkmanship. And we saw it in a pandemic that has forced us to reckon with historical inequalities and injustices. We have allowed big cracks to grow in our national foundation—and what's worse, they feel like they're getting bigger in no small part because of our almost reflexive cynical resignation and inaction.

So, instead of showing up, we often check out. Instead of owning our common challenges, we hunt for someone to blame. We practice consumerism, but not citizenship. Instead of engaging in a politics of mutual trust, we give up our precious capacity for critical thinking. We hand it over to pundits and politicians, whose only job is to convince us of two things: what's wrong with the world, and whose fault it is.

This no-show citizenship creates a vicious cycle. The original indifference of *It's not my problem*, becomes *Boy, that problem is getting worse, somebody ought to do something.* Which eventually metastasizes into *Well, now the problem has grown so big you can't expect me to do anything about it.* Which leads back to *It's not my problem* again. This absolves us of a lot of responsibility from trying to address the biggest issues of our day, from climate change to disinformation destroying our discourse to the seemingly endless struggle against systemic racism.

What if, instead of simply serving as a convenient rhetorical device, *we* truly could mean all of us? Because if, as we learned in school, that *we* are our democracy, then that means every one of our actions, big and small and all taken together, creates our democracy.

We are all co-creators of our collective reality—our interconnected, interdependent, networked reality. And that includes the parts we don't approve of, as well as the stuff we're happy to claim. We can't pick and choose. If *we* are our democracy, then we're just as responsible for the orange-and-yellow flames of burning crosses as we are for the shining gold of our Olympic athletes.

At some point, through either active or benign neglect, we either allowed the civic toxins of cynicism and extreme partisanship and hyper-individualism to spread, or we didn't do enough to stop them—and we have to accept that. If we don't, we'll only continue the anti-democratic cycle. We'll keep casually "otherizing"—holding up ourselves and our like-minded friends as virtuous examples of citizenship while pointing to the problem as those no-show citizens, over there. We'll continue to focus on *they*, not *we*.

Focus on *we*. Use it in your language. And remind yourself and others that in a democracy *we* really does mean everyone. Once this mindset takes hold, it's inevitable that we own issues together, hold ourselves mutually accountable, and put sincere trust in one another. These things are old. They've been with us since the Founding. Together they create the American *we*, and they're waiting for us to reclaim them.

—STEVE SMITH

2

Do Small Acts

Small acts build and sustain democracy. They fortify
our nation's civic fabric, one thread at a time.

IN EARLY 2020, Randy Bretz of Lincoln, Nebraska, saw a
video of people from Spain quarantined on their balconies
cheering for their nation's health-care workers. Bretz, a
retired Nebraska Wesleyan University professor, was moved
by this display of affection—so much so that he resolved
to step out onto his front stoop each night at 8 to clap and
cheer for *his* local health-care workers.

It didn't take long for his neighbors in his middle-class
cul-de-sac to notice, and each evening during that extraordinary spring, more and more of them began to join in.
Soon, the cheering and applause quickly grew into a nightly
neighborhood gathering that lasted far longer than a Tik-
Tok video. Standing six feet apart but together in intent,
neighboring homeowners would take part in the nightly
ritual, then hang around to share everything from home
improvement ideas to the latest COVID-19 tips to news about
family and friends.

Little by little, neighbors got to know one another. New friendships formed; existing ones deepened. The city's mayor caught wind of the gatherings and dropped in. So did the city's chief of police and the district's representative at the statehouse. Neighbors from nearby blocks occasionally made the short walk over. By the end of the summer, *Reader's Digest* included the cul-de-sac among its "Nicest Places In America 2020." "I never thought it would be something I'd look forward to each night," neighbor Eddie Rodel told the magazine. "Since we've all gotten to know each other more, we've helped each other more."

A few miles west, residents of another Lincoln neighborhood—a denser, working-class area south of the city's downtown—also joined for meaningful change. For decades, this area of the city had been sliced in half by a four-lane thoroughfare carrying some 10,000 cars a day to and from downtown. Over time, the social cohesiveness in the area splintered, and because the street was unsafe to cross, residents were largely sequestered on one side or the other.

Having secured grant funding for community improvements, the city proposed reducing the thoroughfare's lanes from four to three—one in each direction instead of two, plus bicycle lanes and a center turn lane to improve traffic flow. But business interests from outside the neighborhood objected—an organization called the Lincoln Independent Business Association led a campaign against lane reduction. The road, LIBA said, was a main connector for areas to the south and the downtown area to the north. It warned of traffic congestion and jammed-up arterial streets if the plan went forward. A city councilman introduced a resolution to halt the project.

Neighbors in the area had long been assumed to be an unorganized mix of renters, low-income families, immigrants, and university students with no time for or interest in politics. But what happened next changed that. Operating on little more than word of mouth, residents flooded the city with emails, letters, and phone calls in support of the roadwork. Neighborhood businesses and organizations signed on. Having created momentum out of thin air, neighbors got organized and strategized with one another to get the project across the finish line. A few weeks later, at a public hearing to discuss the proposal, residents lined up for hours, sharing personal stories and imploring councilmembers to invest in their neighborhood. By evening's end, city leaders (including the councilman who had introduced the resolution to kill the project) voted unanimously to approve the plan.

These two instances show a self-evident truth: Democracy is prosocial. Our individual acts *compound*—and, if we choose, our acts can serve to fortify civic life by connecting with others in common purpose. This can lead to active, responsible co-creation of our shared democratic reality.

It's not always easy. Increasingly, our society favors individualism and materialism, two things that play to our self-interests at the expense of community. Democracy, with its prosocial communitarianism, calls us to recognize what we all have in common and act accordingly. These acts don't need to make the news. Every time we pick up trash from the sidewalk, keep watch on children playing on our street, attend a neighborhood meeting, volunteer at a local school, or shop locally, we are fortifying our community's civic fabric. Each time we write a letter to the editor, connect with new people, take a first aid class, read a local newspaper, or start a book club, we are contributing to our shared democratic infrastructure.

You may be thinking: Gee, this sounds great. But do any of these goodhearted acts amount to anything in the face of the vast, systemic issues keeping us from true progress? How does civil discourse in a middle-class Midwestern cul-de-sac solve the problem of 100,000 toxic tweets being posted every second? Does reconfiguring a short stretch of a street in a single neighborhood address the generations-long practice of discriminatory zoning and the neglect of inner-city neighborhoods? Shouldn't I focus on bigger, more impactful things?

The answer, of course, is *Yes*. The answer is also *You don't have to choose one or the other*. Of the estimated 35,000 decisions we human beings make every day, it's natural to focus on our choices that will make a large impact. That doesn't preclude us from consistently doing smaller, prosocial acts. Sometimes, we have an opportunity to fortify our civic fabric by the bolt; other times, by a few threads. Both are important in the grand scheme of things.

Small acts remind us of our responsibility to one another. Small acts compel us to be engaged in our environments.

Small acts highlight every one of our unique, individual roles in our shared democracy. One by one, little by little, small acts add up.

As a system, America is vast, chaotic, diverse, and complex. But every system has its tipping point. When enough small acts ripple outward, then meaningful, systemic change isn't just possible. It's probable.

—STEVE SMITH

3

Connect with Others

Human connection is the lifeblood of democracy,
binding us tightly to our friends, family,
neighbors, and community. When we direct
our social capital toward a common goal, we
create the condition for meaningful change.

IN EVERY COMMUNITY, everyone has something to contribute. It makes sense, then, that we are called to build networks that connect our gifts to the benefit of our community. For many people, this process is social. Meeting people and building social capital allows our gifts, alongside what others offer, to help create a powerful force.

Social capital equates to a system of relationships and goodwill among people with the influence, authority, or ability to move communities forward. It's a spirit of cooperation with others that forms engagement on community initiatives—to invest our time, talent, and treasure just because someone asked us. Social capital is an eagerness to help, which develops because we have taken the time to build and cultivate relationships. This creates a reserve of generosity in our communities.

When we know someone, we are more likely to trust, help, and listen to them. Just as physical capital is essential to run a successful business, social capital creates opportunities as we work toward common goals. Social capital is a critical element of community progress because it benefits the people between whom it is created and the community in which it lives.

There are many ways to build relationships and create connections. Here are but a few.

Get comfortable with introductions. When we take the time to connect with people and learn about them, we create a connection that can support future community growth. Make time for introductions. Take the time to meet people and learn about them and what they care about.

Cultivate a reputation for showing up and getting things done. People want to work with others who are dependable and hardworking. Once others understand they can count on us, they are more likely to invite us to participate in future work, creating another link in our relationship chain.

Be willing to say yes. In creating a relationship network, say yes to invitations to participate in community efforts, boards, and organizations. This helps to learn about organizations and issues and the people connected to them. It also enables us to solidify what we care about, what our gifts are, and how we can best use them. At the same time, we help others learn about us and how we fit into the fabric of community life.

Become community-focused. Building social capital to serve our community is different from building social capital to benefit an individual career. If we place our shared lives together at the center of our relationship-building, we will form genuinely beneficial connections that can strengthen and grow our community.

Be grateful. As relationships and connections begin to develop, express gratitude. Gratitude strengthens bonds between people, deepens trust, and expands social capital. People want to be around others who see them, appreciate them, and value their contributions. We are more likely to say yes to people who have taken the time to say thank-you to us.

Return the favor. Just as we rely on others early on to introduce us to different groups, invite us to participate in community projects, or help us learn about community needs, so too will others rely on us. Part of being in the relationships that social capital creates means using our unique social capital to help others.

Invite people to participate. Just as we must be willing to leverage our social capital for the common good, we must also be willing to help others build relationship networks. Build a network of those who are ready and willing to contribute to a life together by continuously inviting new people to participate. Creating a broader network of relationships makes community success more likely.

Building relationships, connections, and social capital takes time. But communities with strong relationship networks have less infighting, more collaboration, and are more likely to get things done. Working together eliminates territorial issues and competition for resources and increases the chance of solving issues. As we make connections across our communities, they become stronger. We forge tighter bonds. And we build a powerful foundation to sustain them—one person, one place, one issue at a time.

—TAMMY DAY

4

Give Up the Right to Remain Silent

Democracy is noisy. Do not just "go along" to be polite.
Standing out and speaking up challenges the status quo
and protects everyone against the threat of oppression.

IN THE STUDY OF COMMUNICATION, there is a theory
known as the "Spiral of Silence." Humans dread isolation
and rejection, the theory goes, and so we often stay quiet
instead of voicing our opinions, for fear we will be seen as
having views that might run counter to dominant opinion.
The "Spiral of Silence" assumes that in any given situation,
we can discern what the prevailing opinion is and then react
accordingly. It was first employed to explain why Germans
did not talk about the rise of the Nazis and their atrocities.
The "spiral" is created—and the silence is echoed—when
members of the self-professed majority confidently voice
what they believe is the dominant opinion. Those who
believe they have minority views fear being shunned and
become increasingly uncomfortable. As the spiral continues,
the hesitation, silence, and fear deepen.

Even amid accelerating disruption and fragmentation in
our cultural, political, and social climate, this "spiral" is still

at work. The mass media cast a powerful image of prevailing opinion, as do social platforms like Facebook, Twitter, and Instagram. Meanwhile, in real space, we carefully navigate the landscapes of our workplaces, schools, houses of worship, and anywhere our social networks (both formal and informal) take shape. While dominant opinion can certainly shift in times of upheaval, such as the protest-filled summer of 2020, it is dominant for a reason. It is formidable and self-justifying. Plus, our social customs tend to reward civility—from the genteel etiquette of the South to Midwestern charm—and discourage aggression. This is good news for those who support the status quo.

Still, nowhere does the Constitution give the powerful interests an absolute right to impose their worldview on the rest of us. Just as our founding document protects against majoritarian hegemony on behalf of the minority, it empowers us—beseeches us—to not just go along with the crowd. It implores us to be individuals, to advocate for our beliefs, to stand up and stand out, and to inspire others to do the same. For democracy to flourish, we must work to shatter the "spiral."

It is important to consider that *the "spiral" may actually be the product of perception and not reality*. This often comes to the fore when a majority opinion is challenged. In fact, it may only have become the accepted wisdom because its purveyors were more persistent and louder than the rest. Things are often not what they seem, and standing up and speaking out inspires others to do so, too.

It is also essential that we *use our own words*. Popular culture, especially TV and film, is full of passionate speech-making and eloquent entreaties changing the course of history. But we don't have to employ the eloquent rhetoric of Atticus Finch in *To Kill a Mockingbird*, nor do we need to show the care and heartache of Jefferson Smith on the Senate floor in *Mr. Smith Goes to Washington*. When we use our own words, we are more likely to connect with our neighbors and community members more genuinely. Whether it's testimony before the City Council, a letter to the editor, or a social media post that urges people to consider something beyond the dominant framework, we can successfully challenge the status quo.

We must also *reinforce, reinforce, and reinforce again*. For most, going out on a limb once can be plenty frightening. Doing it repeatedly might be unthinkable. But, repetition is absolutely necessary to speak up and stand out; messages must be repeated over and over to take hold in our consciousness. It's only human nature that any message or opinion, no matter how potent, will fade without repetition and reinforcement. A ridiculously obvious example: Think of commercials for the insurance company Aflac. Its mascot, a white duck, has been quacking the company's name in advertisements for more than two decades now. According to the company, nine in 10 Americans now recognize Aflac's brand. If the choice is between a clever, complicated message and a simple, repeatable one, we will always choose the latter.

Of course, we should also keep in mind that *the majority opinion might really be the majority opinion*. Yet, this does not mean we should pack things up and simply concede our principles. If we truly find ourselves counter to prevailing winds, whether it be at a town hall meeting or in a Facebook thread, messages can be tailored so that they are more empathetic and more palatable. It also forces us to find common ground with those with whom we disagree. Over time, this leads to trust, which leads to connection, which leads to empathy, which leads to compromise and even change.

And, of course, we should *expect pushback*. Unfortunately, in recent years our leaders have given us permission to communicate from our worst impulses. Speaking up and standing out can be dangerous when the powerful feel their authority or hegemony has been challenged. They may retreat to calls for "civility" while casting themselves as victims of aggressive words or actions, but they are just as likely to use their power to overwhelm, demean, or even call for violence against others. In every interaction we must use our best judgment and recognize when discretion is the better part of valor.

Ideas are contagious, and in a democracy—the most adaptive, flexible, and re-inventable system in human history—the exchange of ideas is absolutely necessary. If we remain silent we surrender the intellectual marketplace to those who do not share our experiences or represent our views. They may even have a distaste for democracy itself.

But by speaking up, we can cast away the illusion of the established order, bring a plurality of ideas to the forefront, and make meaningful change possible. Sometimes, we can even change the world.

—STEVE SMITH

Conversation Starters: Community

* What empowers you about your community?

* Who are the local difference-makers that you know?

* Who in your community do you look up to?

* What community assets, gifts, or strengths support civic structures that promote building of networks both formal and informal?

* What businesses or organizations embody community values important to you?

* What is unique about your community that makes it stand out?

* What places or events in your community share space or stories to bring people together?

PART TWO

Choose Learning

Learning creates pathways to participation and progress. In all its forms, study and instruction and education strengthens our communities and us.

5

Be Political

> We are all in the political arena, whether we want
> to be or not. Ignoring politics is in fact a political
> act, in the sense that we concede our right to
> others to affect your world for good or for ill.

THESE DAYS, "POLITICS" IS A DIRTY WORD. Who can blame reasonable people for being averse to endless partisan drama, ideological mendacity, and party-line gridlock? Especially because when it comes to politicians, more is always said than is ever done. "Nothing really changes," says the self-avowed apolitical American. "So why bother with any of it?"

There is a comfort in declaring oneself *apolitical*. It's nice to consider ourselves above what we see as petty squabbles at the Capitol, the Statehouse, or City Hall. This allows us to airlock politics from our lives until we absolutely have to summon it again. Every two or four years, we might crack open the hatch, briefly step out and blacken a few ovals, then seal off that segment of our lives again until the next Election Day.

And yet, politics is everywhere, whether we want it to be or not. And we all are inherently political creatures, whether we want to be or not.

Despite the popular definition that causes such revulsion, politics is not just the narrow actions of Beltway insiders. Politics is our realm of public life. It's where Americans of diverse backgrounds, ideals, and opinions work, directly or indirectly, to shape our society. We all participate in politics, whether we know it or not: What we buy, who we agree with, who we disagree with, our daily discussions, our donations and volunteer hours, every daily act that favors the common good or advances our individual interests—all of these are political acts.

Consider an "average day" in America. Everything from the resources we expend to the physical infrastructure we share to the worker and consumer protections we enjoy is the result of someone at some point asking, *Why are things like this?* and then championing ideas to make them better. These ideas may have seemed radical or unattainable at the time. Ask those who advocated for the 40-hour work week, or clean drinking water, or strict public health standards, or safety benchmarks for housing, roads, and bridges, or protections for consumers. Once, these obvious elements of modern society were controversial ideas being batted around the public square.

The irony of politics being everywhere all the time is that it's easy to overlook how profoundly it has affected us over time. Part of this is by design: Because our democratic republic is built to favor moderate and incremental change, meaningful progress often requires persistence and patience. Sometimes, by the time an idea grows from a proposal to a bill to a law to—eventually—an indelible and essential part of American life, we've likely forgotten that it was originally the product of our politics.

Claiming to be apolitical is to announce we are settling for the world as it currently is. Maybe that's a result of our privilege, our assumption that politics can't affect us thanks to our incomes or our social status. Or maybe it's because of a disdain for the saturation coverage of the *maneuvering* of our politics every day on CNN, Fox News, and MSNBC. Or perhaps, at long last, we've simply been conditioned to believe in our modern political environment that "just OK" is the best we can hope for.

Be wary of this trap. The myth of apoliticalism gives rise to other, more dangerous notions, such as politics being one of a number of "channels" that Americans can choose based on their tastes. Or the fantastical idea that politics should never bleed into these other "channels," such as sports, entertainment, or art. History has proven time and again the folly of this thinking: In recent years, the words and actions of athletes like Colin Kaepernick, Megan Rapinoe, and LeBron James, or artists such as The Chicks, Neil Young, and Killer Mike—have highlighted the fallacy of the "channel," just as Tommie Smith, John Carlos, Muhammad Ali, and Woody Guthrie did before them.

At our very core, humans are aspirational and curious creatures. And as Americans, we pride ourselves on achieving The American Dream by being hard-wired to constantly evaluate our current state, envision how we can improve our lot for ourselves and our children, and then going out and doing something about it. Yes, ingenuity and hard work are important parts of this process. But politics is the lens through which that better world can be seen and organized for ourselves and others.

The good news is that we don't have to run for elected office or become a gadfly at the State Capitol to practice politics. Nor do we have to enlist in the never-ending hyper-partisan wars that turn so many people away from our democratic processes. We can begin by simply being politically aware: We can learn more about the issues that we already care about; that knowledge, in turn, allows us to seek entry points into our politics to positively affect our shared democratic reality.

Where we shop (or don't shop), where and how we travel, our very methods of commuting, where we choose to live and send our kids to school, what organizations we support—all are political acts. They are worthy of our conscious reflection and, taken together with the reflection and actions of others, can build a framework for meaningful change.

"The people who say that they have not time to attend to politics are simply saying that they are unfit to live in a free community," Teddy Roosevelt once said. Nothing happens in isolation. So be political. Better yet, let's recognize the self-evident fact that we already *are*.

—STEVE SMITH

6

Read

Reading is an act of engaged democratic citizenship. It builds empathy and character, expands knowledge, and encourages critical thought. Reading keeps us free.

IGNORANCE IS NOT BLISS. Ignorance is a constant and real threat to democracy. Democratic societies demand an informed populace, because when we cultivate knowledge and a better understanding of our world we are inevitably motivated to improve it. That's human nature, and it's been proven time and time again in the United States.

It's no wonder, then, that authoritarians fear an educated citizenry. The greater a country's intellectual and cultural isolation, the more susceptible it is to propaganda and disinformation. History is replete with attempts to eradicate or suppress information that runs counter to a regime's established orthodoxy—from Nazi Germany's book burnings to today's Great Firewall of China, which blocks "politically troublesome" websites, to every aspect of life in the "Hermit Kingdom" of North Korea. Authoritarians can't stay in power if people have the means to access new evidence, critically assess it, be influenced by a range of other thinkers, and ultimately conceive a better world.

Simply put, if people know *how* to think, then they can't be told *what* to think.

Reading keeps us free by building within us the essential instruments of self-government. Not only does reading sharpen our civic skills, it is the core act of engaged democratic citizenship—and it always will be, even as YouTube, TikTok, and Instagram trim away our attention spans.

Yes, the culture that created the phrase "TL;DR (Too Long; Didn't Read)" is less likely to read and reflect. And yes, it's often easier to watch a video than read a news article or to eschew the book in favor of its film adaptation. The quaint notion of reading may seem outmoded in the fast-forward world of the 21st century. And yet, there remains no substitute for the written word in the marketplace of ideas. Reading words that constitute important new ideas (and not watching them flicker across a screen or listening to them in a podcast) is critical to our social, educational, and democratic growth as individuals.

But why exactly is reading central to democracy? First, it builds *empathy*, which gives us the ability to imagine and respond to lives that are different from our own. Without empathy, our society would devolve into the chaos of hyper-individualism, and the democratic promise of equality for all people could not be realized.

Second, reading builds *character*, which compels us to understand and protect the principles upon which our nation was founded. These values—honesty, fairness, self-restraint—inform us Americans about how to improve our systems, treat one another, and honor our democratic traditions. Character drives our pursuit of a more perfect union.

Third, reading expands *knowledge*, which shapes our understanding of the complexity and nuance of our world, its history, its persistent questions and its eternal conflicts. For democracy to work, we must understand the context in which it exists and actively engage in it. This civic knowledge goes beyond how our government and political systems work; it also includes our rights, roles, and responsibilities as Americans. Or in the words of James Madison: "a popular government, without popular information or the means of acquiring it, is but a prologue to a farce or a tragedy."

And finally, reading develops *critical thought*—how to access information, analyze it for its veracity and, above all, to become well-intentioned skeptics in our increasingly saturated communications landscape. In the Information Age, critical thinking has emerged as an urgent and relevant democratic skill. "Fake news" threatens to undercut our ability to confront shared challenges because it undercuts our ability to identify a set of shared facts. Citizen readers, however, can recognize such propaganda, baseless conspiracy theories, and demagoguery—and reject it.

When we open a book or news article, we enter a space as solemn and private as the voting booth. Once in this space, we often employ our imaginative capacity to put ourselves in another's shoes. At the same time, we remind ourselves of our personal choices that have led us to this particular space at this particular time. This internal monologue is occurring to you right now, as you engage with this book. "That inner self," said Azar Nafisi, an Iranian-American writer, reflecting on active and reflective reading, "is what makes it possible for private individuals to become responsible citizens of their country and of the world, linking their own good to that of their society, becoming active and informed participants. For this they need to know, to pause, to think, to question."

Our society is safer and stronger because of our collective freedom to read. Our right to evaluate ideas—and to organize and scrutinize them amid the unfettered flow of public information—is precious. We must exercise this right to the fullest. To truly realize a modern and robust democracy, first we must read. Then we must reflect. And then we must act.

—STEVE SMITH

7

Empty Your Pockets

> Our civil society is not judged by how neatly
> we agree. It is judged by how we can disagree
> so passionately and so personally and yet still
> carry out our American experiment. This takes
> courage, but it is essential to democracy.

IN *THE BIG SORT*, Bill Bishop discusses at length how in the mid-1970s, Americans began clustering into more and more granular communities of sameness. This "Big Sort," he wrote, was happening simultaneously as other social and economic changes in America.

To understand what effect this has had on our modern democracy, let's zoom back to 1976, our Bicentennial year. We'd be surprised at how different civic life looked compared to today. There were Elks Clubs, Jaycees, American Legions and Legion Auxiliaries; the pews were packed in our Lutheran and Methodist churches, and newspapers were on nearly every doorstep. Walmart was still almost a decade away from setting foot in Nebraska—so our Main Streets still had appliance dealers, clothing shops, dime stores, and hardware stores. Plus, all the interaction that went with all of that. Our commercial centers were still civic centers.

Here's the gist of what happened: Increasingly toward the end of the 20th Century, Americans became more broadly affluent, and that increased our options in all facets of life. Gradually and with the help of technology, the old institutions around land, family, class, tradition—even religion— began to give way. In their place, a new order based on the notion of individual choice emerged. The era of hyper-individualism was upon us.

Today, some neighborhoods are concentrated with foreign-car-driving, HBO-watching, Fair Trade-coffee drinking, dual-income-no-kids households. A few blocks away, three-car driveways have Ford F-150s in them, and *Blue Bloods* and *Live PD* are on the TV. Chick-Fil-A takeout is on the table and on Sundays, those folks fill a nearby megachurch.

And that's just in the *physical* world. We're spending more and more time in our virtual Pockets, which has accelerated the divide. Bill Bishop wrote *The Big Sort* in 2008, just as Facebook and Twitter were hitting the mainstream. Ever since, social media has tightened its grip on nearly every aspect of our lives—particularly in a pandemic, with our screens suddenly becoming the safest way to interact with one another across an infinite spectrum of experiences. And yet, we don't.

Social scientists call this *assortative behavior*. Birds of a feather flock together—or in this case, fragmenting and splintering and filtering into like-minded groups. We call it "Pocket Democracy."

You might be thinking, Is this an entirely bad thing? In a world that is literally on fire, what's wrong with retreating to a safe place? Why is being around people I like, who share my sensibilities, and who will let me drop my guard for a little while, a bad thing?

Birds of a feather flock together, right?

It's what happens within the flock that weakens democracy. You'd think that the safety of being in a strictly like-minded community would bring a kind of peace and confidence—a refuge. But it's mostly the opposite. More often than not, we become more extreme in these homogeneous environments. Lock-stepped groups create a self-justifying feedback loop. In the case of our interactions in our Pockets, this means an unspoken competition of sorts to be the brightest Red or deepest Blue member of our chosen group.

Pocket democracies grow on moral certitude and ideological purity. In a Pocket democracy, we are not self-governing individuals; we don't make our choices as the result of careful research or after coming to a well-informed opinion. We cast them as an after-the-fact affirmation, a confirmation of our status within our chosen group. Along the way, we leave a lot of wreckage: Friendships end. Family relationships get strained. Workplaces become divided.

To address that longing for connection and common purpose, and to return to what unites us, we must be civic actors and not passive consumers of a Pocket democracy, one that's conveniently tailor-made for our specific beliefs. To be clear, we're not saying to chum up to white supremacists in a sincere attempt to understand where they're coming from. In a democracy built on equality, inclusion, and love, certain moral boundaries remain non-negotiable. And we're not saying that Americans shouldn't be partisan. Be partisan and be political, whatever that means to you personally. Part of being active, responsible citizens is to publicly lend support to—and to work for—the candidates and causes that we believe in. This isn't a call to get a political lobotomy.

But we must empty our Pockets and meaningfully communicate with Americans with whom we disagree. This takes courage. Our society, politics, and culture have made it too easy to choose not to act. Plus, the less we interact with those who don't think or pray or vote like us, the more distrustful we become. We believe the worst in one another and we genuinely believe the "other side" is more extreme and radical than it really is. We reduce people to caricature.

How do we break free of our Pockets? First, know this: Despite all the noise in our echo chambers and all they do to distort our view of others, our perceptions are not necessarily reality. We Americans still tend to be more alike than we think.

Research tends to confirm this. Take immigration, for example. In a 2019 study by the nonpartisan group More in Common, Republicans said they believed that seven in 10 Democrats supported completely open borders. In reality, fewer than four in 10 do. And, not to be outdone, in that same study Democrats believed that maybe half of Republicans think immigration is good for America. The actual support among average Republicans is eight in 10. One set of numbers adds up to hateful caricature. The other set suggests a much more platonic truth.

This doesn't mean we don't have clear differences. But we are not our caricatures. Remember this when summoning the fortitude to start a difficult conversation outside of your Pocket. Keep this in mind when finding the courage to talk with one another again (and, without abandoning our most cherished and most deeply held beliefs, finding the courage to listen to one another again).

Be brave. For centuries, from our town halls to our statehouses, from our high-school gyms to our water coolers, Americans have gathered, listened to each other, debated, made up our minds, and then moved forward as one.

We've done it before. We can do it again.

—STEVE SMITH

8

Argue Like an American

Democracy is forged in our discourse. It is sustained
through our discussions. And it is advanced by
honest dialogue and in the exchange of ideas and
opinions. Our nation was founded on an argument
and it's our responsibility to continue it.

WELL-MEANING AND REASONABLE PEOPLE HAVE SPENT
recent years begging their friends, family, and more than a
few elected officials to embrace "civil discourse." Some folks
are asking for peace, some for quiet, others for a space to
have tough conversations. Most popular writing about civil
discourse unmistakably emphasises the first word—*civil*.
It's taken for granted that we know how to discourse, and
popular opinion is nearly unanimous that we could all use
some help with the civil part.

But our problem is not with being civil. Our problem is
that we don't know what we mean when we say *discourse*.
Discourse is argument. They're not just similar, they're two
words for the same thing. Discourse comes from the latin
word *discursus*, which literally means "an argument." If
we're going to improve our collective ability to engage in

civil discourse, we must first confront fundamental problems with how we think about, talk about, and respond to argument.

The language we use to talk about our society is almost exclusively the language of building. Language is our toolbox with which we do the building. Argument is the most essential and most frequently used tool, and we spend most of our time pretending like we're not using it, at the cost of our effectiveness, relationships, and even our health. But we all tinker, build, tear down, and rebuild. Like any primate on any project, we use tools to accomplish those tasks. Argument is, on both a small and large scale, one of the defining tools of our society.

Americans neither invented nor own argument-as-tool, but it is certainly one of the more readily available tools in our toolbox. Our most prized civic possessions are arguments put to paper—the Declaration of Independence is an argument for why King George lost the right to govern American colonists and a justification for the new path we new friends were taking. The Constitution is an argument for what a government needs to do to "establish justice, ensure domestic tranquility, provide for the common defence, promote the general welfare, and secure the blessings of liberty to ourselves and our posterity." Nearly everyone has used argument as a tool to advocate for good, to justify evil, to demand inclusion or independence, and to promote a product or a philosophy. Argument co-creates meaning with other people. Without it, we'd just be a bunch of bumbling word-sayers live-laugh-loving our way through the world with a severely limited capacity for making meaning.

We don't often think about argument as a tool because it's so ingrained in our way of being, so instinctual, at this point. Sometimes wielding an unseen tool like argument is conscious; most of the time, it's not. And while there's nothing wrong with instinctually or subconsciously using tools to accomplish our goals, there are a few basic principles that even the most experienced tinkerer would do well to remember.

Tools are value neutral. There is nothing inherently good or evil about a hammer. There is nothing inherently good or evil about argument. All tools can be used or misused, squandered or used to have maximum impact. One of the most foundational dangers to the long-term health of our civil discourse is our predisposition against argument. Argument is usually associated with negative connotations. Calling someone "argumentative" signals that they are stubborn and taxing to be around. Our rules against politics and religion at the dinner table have nothing to do with politics and religion but the arguments they tend to invite. Argumentative children are bad children. Someone who argues just for the sake of challenging ideas is called a "devil's advocate." We are taught that argument is evil, to be avoided, and not something to celebrate or practice.

Having been raised to understand argument as morally wrong and a punishable offense, we grow up and can't for the life of us understand why we fight with our partners, have awkward miscommunications with our friends, feel discontent at work, and continue electing an incompetent Congress whose defining characteristic is its inability to function.

Underpinning much of our misbelief about argument is the false assumption that argument always (and only) serves one function: the function of rebellion, or defiance, or opposition. This is often true, both on the individual and societal level. The Declaration was, among other things, a proclamation of rebellion. But the important part of that last sentence is the least obvious part—"among other things." The Declaration was a declaration of rebellion. A voter calling their senator to express concern over a vote is an act of opposition. A young child resisting bedtime is an act of defiance. But they are not *only* those things. They are all, to varying degrees and to varying consequences, seeking to understand, trying to inform, asking for help, questioning assumptions, making assumptions, expressing needs, testing boundaries, challenging authority, exploring their relationship to that authority, claiming territory, and aspiring to a world they think, in that moment, is better.

Arguments are doing all of those things, all of the time. And the more aware we become of this versatility, the more difficult it becomes to dismiss arguments with the hollow moralizing many of us were shown as children, instead embracing the rich messiness of communicating with people we value about ideas we value.

Are there ways to argue more effectively, more persuasively, in a way that can make you a "better" arguer? Sure.

We'd all benefit from an improved awareness of sound argument structure, social cues to know whether now is really the time to say this thing on our minds, and knowing how certain tones will or won't serve us with a particular audience. But conflating efficacy with morality is another common mistake hindering us in our quest for more effective civil discourse.

Most of us have a shared understanding of the "correct way" to use a hammer. But what if someone decides to use a hammer in a weird, unusual way? What if they use it to smash a marshmallow, or put a dent in their workbench, just because they feel like it? Is that wrong? Of course not. There would be practical consequences—a dented workbench and probably nobody willing to linger while they make really loud noises, but the hammerer is well within their rights to dent the workbench and live with the consequences.

It's difficult to hear everyone from politicians to parents telling someone that they "can't" argue in a certain way. Of course they can. It won't make them very well-liked by the person they're protesting, and it probably won't give them much access to short-term influence with that person. But who says that's the point? The folks who believe they have a monopoly on the proper function or form of argument are usually the folks who wield "civility" like a weapon in a way that is, at best, tone-policing and dismissive—and at worst, violent and blatant racism.

One of the most dangerous consequences of our predisposition against argument is the belief that argument is something you can choose not to do. Argument is everywhere. If you are in any way attempting to influence another person's perception, attitude, or beliefs, you are engaging in argument. This can be as obvious as arguing with your dad about the president or as subtle as trying to cheer up a friend. We are all arguing all of the time. But the stronger our ingrained distaste for argument, the harder we pretend that we're doing something besides arguing. And there is simply no way that using a tool while pretending we're doing something else gives us access to the healthiest, most effective, best version of that tool.

We don't always have to like it. We want people to like us and many of us feel other people's discomfort with argument, especially obvious arguments (i.e. politics and religion) deeply. But whichever layer of society you're concerned with, you are engaging in some kind of building metaphor—and argument is a tool you simply can't afford to not use. Is your focus on building meaningful friendships? The very notion of authenticity is an honest presentation of your core argument: "this is me." Building a professional network? You are constantly engaging in arguments about the very definition of words like "professionalism," "good work," and "fair compensation," and you are performing your understanding of those words in a way that is defended, criticized, and renegotiated at every turn. Engaging in politics? Campaigning? Voting? You are engaging in some of the largest and most foundational arguments about the direction of our nation, the competency of elected officials, as you argue for your definition of "the right direction" for the country, state, city, or neighborhood.

It would be hypocritical to write about the harms of moralizing arguments, then tell you that you *must engage in argument*. And to splice the various times when certain people's participation may or may not be morally required is beyond the scope of this little essay. But it seems a fact that if you don't engage in argument then you will simply be a passenger. Your life, both daily and as a whole, will be dictated to you by others, and you will watch others' lives be dictated to them. If you really aren't arguing, you will have no option but to look at change in the world—change for good, change for evil, advances and setbacks—and simply nod your head and say, "this is so." And that is fundamentally out of step with the spirit that both started and sustains our nation.

—WESTIN MILLER

9
Supplant the Media Slant

Separate the signal from the noise. Be wary of
the information that is coming to you on your
phone, your screen, and over the airwaves.

INFORMATION IS POWER. We need it to make educated
decisions as we navigate life. But, we must challenge ourselves to think deeper about the media we consume. Misin-
formation and disinformation campaigns are increasingly
everywhere and we must be prepared to identify falsehoods,
verify truths, and protect ourselves from too much news.

We know firsthand how fatiguing the news cycle can be.
From the endless comments, push notifications, social feeds,
emails, and more. Yet, it is important that we stay informed.
So how can we stay in the loop while also maintaining
our sanity?

First, we must evaluate our sources. Think about where we
get our news. Why do we follow a particular news source?
Did we deliberately choose those outlets or were they given
to us? Many of us inherit our media preferences and information sources from our family, friends, and peers. If our
parents always watched a certain local news channel, we are

more likely to watch that station because it is familiar, not always because it is the best or most informative.

When evaluating our sources, we can ask ourselves what it is we are seeking. Do we want the most accurate and concise coverage of an issue? Or, do we want information that agrees with us, and our personal worldviews? When we are taking stock of the media's perspective, we should be sure to reflect on our own. Also, we can consider the messenger; for instance, if all the news we read comes from reporters of one race, gender, socioeconomic background, and so on, we are not getting multiple perspectives on an issue or story.

Depending on our environment, our choice in news can be limited—particularly in rural and low-income communities where internet access and diverse media outlets can be scarcer. It's important to take note that whatever we are hearing is not the entire truth. We must search for other sources of information to broaden our awareness.

Second, we must consider the format. There are so many ways to consume news and information today: TV, radio, newspaper, social media, text messages, word of mouth, yard signs, posters, mailers—you name it. We are the most connected humans in human history, and we have the most access to the most information, ever, at our fingertips. It is so important to understand that *how* we receive information is just as, if not more, significant than the core message.

Marshall McLuhan, a Canadian philosopher and communications theorist in the 1960s, famously said *The medium is the message*. That means that how we communicate has a profound impact on our comprehension of the world. How we get our news can shape what we take from it. For example, when newspapers dominated the landscape in the 18th, 19th and 20th centuries, audiences received information about their world when the paper landed on their doorstep. Now, as soon as something happens it is shared via social media and can be recapped, remixed, and modified a thousand times over within just a few minutes. The significance of the information can be distorted, amplified, or reduced because of where it is coming from.

Diversifying our news sources makes us more engaged and better informed. So if we get most of our news from social media, we can and should try finding a podcast, listening to a radio story, picking up a newspaper, or visiting specific news sites. We can also try following a variety of online sources to fact-check what we are learning.

Finally, we must get offline and go "outside." So much of our perspective of the world is shaped by our media consumption that we rarely take time to go outside and see how things are actually happening. This is especially important in a time of civil unrest. News coverage, social media posts, and second-hand accounts of protests and rallies can skew how events transpired. Though we can't be everywhere at all times, especially during a pandemic, we ought to do our best to get a firsthand account of what is happening around us. If the news tells us it is raining while we are inside sucked into our phones, we're more likely to believe it than if you went outside to confirm for ourselves.

This analogy and advice do have a flaw—that is, what we perceive is not always the truth, because our perception is limited. So, just because we saw something a certain way, does not mean we have all the facts to come to an absolutely clear conclusion. Our perspective is just that, ours, and learning the perspectives of others helps us build a more accurate representation of what is happening. We can't just go outside physically, but mentally, too.

There is so much to be aware of at this time. Information bombards us at all times—and not all of it is designed to enlighten us. It takes vigilance to separate the signal from the noise. It requires us to think a little deeper about how and why things are the way they are. Mass media have a major influence on our worldview and it is incumbent upon us to validate and challenge what we see to better understand it.

By identifying, verifying, and diversifying our news, we do the work of fortifying the fabric of our shared democratic reality.

—DAWAUNE HAYES

10

Reject Untruth

*Without the creation, understanding, and sharing
of facts, democracy dies. Oppose public lying
in all its forms and be a partisan for truth.*

UNTRUTH MATTERS. On January 6, 2021, we gained a deep appreciation of just how much. A mob of insurrectionists, whipped into a frenzy by the sitting president, stormed our nation's legislative chambers and halted the certification of his successor's electoral win. At the U.S. Capitol doors, the mob chanted for the sitting vice president to be hanged. Others called for kidnapping or assassinating our elected leaders. Insurrectionists ransacked and looted Congressional offices, stole and damaged property and paraded the Stars and Bars through the Capitol halls. Shots were fired. Blood was spilled. A police officer was bludgeoned and later died from his injuries. Another was dragged down the Capitol steps and beaten. And as the world watched in horror, the citadel of the world's oldest democracy fell into the hands of seditionists.

The only way for us to truly reckon with the catastrophe that unfolded in the U.S. Capitol on January 6 is through the logical evaluation of these self-evident facts. Common sense tells us these were criminal acts. But they also were much more. They were the catastrophic endpoint of the intentional weaponization of lies—untruths designed to destroy our confidence in our democratic institutions.

Simply put, democracy will not survive if the number of Americans who refuse to acknowledge shared facts—a number that is currently in the minority—becomes the majority. There will be no realm of public life, no space in which we all compete and cooperate for resources, rights, responsibilities, and ideals. There will be no collective social process to build our society. When facts are regularly degraded into untruths, and those untruths fuel those angry or misguided enough to supplant the power of ballots with the power of bullets, democracy is done.

In the case of January 6, 2021, the perverted facts involved the most important truths in American democracy: the results of a free and fair election. Voting is a sacred process; through it, citizens in a democratic society collectively transform their convictions, values, and views into reality. The casting, accepting, counting, announcing, and certifying of our ballots creates the *will of the people*, the most powerful of democratic truths. Yet for several months after the 2020 presidential election, the forces of untruth relentlessly degraded the facts that Americans had formed with their ballots. They flooded the public sphere with lies that the election had been stolen, despite overwhelming evidence to the contrary. Through it all, they aimed to reverse-engineer established facts back into beliefs.

They were laughed out of court and rebuffed by impartial election officials. Nevertheless, they persisted. In many corners, untruth not only prevailed but dominated. Ultimately it manifested into a literal assault on American democracy. Unfortunately, that gray January day was far from unexpected: For too long, the forces of untruth have waged war on our public discourse. For too long, their toxic messages have found too many eager ears. The untruths continue today.

Truth, unwavering and unbending, is independent of political belief. So we must do everything in our power to keep revisionism of that awful day's facts from ever taking hold. The facts of January 6 are too important to be bent into anti-democratic beliefs. Going forward, we must loudly and aggressively reject untruth, in every form and whenever we encounter it.

Passively acknowledging untruths and failing to loudly and roundly condemn them brought us a mob that crashed through barricades, stormed the Capitol, and called for the murder of our elected officials. Whether we were there on the front lines or merely watching from the safety of our homes, we all bear responsibility for this.

The facts of January 6 are not kind. They do not make us feel good about ourselves. It's human nature to want to look away, distance ourselves, and rationalize how the assault on the Capitol could have happened. But we must accept the facts. And by accepting them, we can find power in them—*because facts have power.* We must respect that power and we must be partisans for truth. In the long run, only facts and truth can enable us to rebuild a mutual respect that guards against future threats to our democracy. Only in mutual acceptance of stubborn facts will we find the will to move forward. And part of moving forward means we must look back at January 6 and say: *Never again.*

—STEVE SMITH

Conversation Starters: Learning

* From what sources do you get most of your news?
* How do you inform yourself of candidates' or officials' positions on the issues?
* What books, articles, or essays have had the most lasting effects on your worldview?
* What is the best way to react when you are confronted with an obvious untruth?
* Do you have friendships with people from other generations?
* What's the difference between politeness and civility?

PART THREE

Choose Empowerment

*Power is inherent in every person,
and anyone can lead change in their
community. Connecting people to power
is our democracy's secret weapon.*

11

Claim & Spread Civic Power

Power isn't just reserved for elites. Anyone
can claim, exercise, and share civic power,
and create meaningful change.

IN THIS HYPERPARTISAN AGE, it's not all that surprising
that a lot of our focus and attention is on the acquisition,
nature, and use of power. Power shows up everywhere in
national headlines: a constant drip-drip-drip about how it
is wielded by government actors, about how it's separated
in our Constitution, about how a particular political figure
is nakedly pursuing it, or about how it is transferred from
one administration to another.

This kind of power—state-based and governmental—is
and always should be the subject of close scrutiny. But this
is not the only kind of power being practiced in the United
States. Large corporations, businesses that dominate local
or regional economies, well-resourced institutions and
advocacy groups, and individuals with wealth, pedigree, or
connections all work to amplify a self-perpetuating narrative
that says power is reserved only for the elected, appointed,
or privileged few.

We can accept this paradigm, or we can address it as the illusion that it is. All Americans, regardless of station or background, are entitled to power. And of all the different brands of power, the kind that citizens wield—civic power—is best at creating meaningful and lasting change. To acquire it, civic power requires no entry fee, no particular birthright, no special favors or tributes. *Anyone* can be a civic actor at *any time*. This, of course, is by design: Democratic power by its very nature is intended to be widely distributed. And throughout our history, our nation has tended to be at its strongest when more of us have had access to the overall share of power.

Civic power collects. It compounds. And, if fully realized, it spreads to new places, energizes, and multiplies. In 1981, President Jimmy Carter touched on the inherent nature of this vast, largely untapped power in his farewell address. "In a few days, I will lay down my official responsibilities in this office," Carter said, "to take up once more the only title in our democracy superior to that of president, the title of citizen."

This might sound quaint these days. Self-proclaimed "realists" contend that there's only so much power to be had; that it can't just be simply claimed or conjured, but *seized* from someone else. And that even if the average American does become motivated to seek power and agency, they'll find all of it except some table crumbs already locked up by elites.

But power is not finite. It is not zero-sum, and most importantly, it is not reserved for the predetermined few. In America, it can be created out of nothing. It can emerge in unlikely places where none previously existed. It can be multiplied, increased, and—most importantly—spread to others in pursuit of common goals. We know this because we've seen it, over and over, in our democracy-building work: citizens who master the methods and use of power by organizing, connecting, and acting. From neighborhood advocacy to nationwide movements, ordinary Americans have rediscovered the infinite well of civic power. You can, too.

To begin, it's necessary to first *understand the landscape of power*. Take the time to form an objective evaluation of your community's structures of power. Ask yourself: Who are the people—elected officials, business leaders, community advocates, others—who really run things? How do they exercise power? To what end? Then ask yourself: Why is this so? How do they maintain power? And, finally: How can this be different? What must happen in order to reshuffle the landscape of power? Research these questions thoroughly. Then, reflect on the answers. This reflection will form the foundation and very framework of your pursuit of civic power.

At some point, you will inevitably move from *reflection to action, and from action to connection*. The very process of seeking answers to the questions above increases the potential for forming and joining networks of like-minded people who happen to be asking similar questions. This civic exercise is fundamentally American: Physical venues such as town halls, neighborhood meetings, marches, or protests have served as ways to connect Americans down through the ages. Today, digital social networking makes it easier than ever for fellow travelers to meet, organize, strategize, and activate *en masse*. During the COVID-19 crisis, non-union "essential workers" across different industries—grocery chains, distribution services, restaurants—flocked to an online platform called Coworker.org to unify around a range of reforms, including better health and safety precautions, hazard pay, and even benefits for part-time workers. It's an example of how a multitude can rewrite political, social, and cultural rules.

As your civic power and platform grow, it is important to *spread it exponentially by telling, sharing, and amplifying stories* that can then motivate and unite others to take up the cause. The power of storytelling allows us to communicate important truths and bring people together with a common purpose. Stories can elevate visibility, fortify collective identity, magnify inequalities and injustices, build political influence, and encourage would-be bystanders to get involved.

Consider the story of Bold Nebraska. In 2010, it formed as a small progressive group on the notion that issues, not ideology, are what drive people to make local change. It ended up successfully battling Big Oil to an international stalemate. When TransCanada proposed building the Keystone XL oil pipeline through Nebraska, Bold Nebraska began a hyperlocal campaign that told the stories of real Nebraskans whose rights and livelihoods would be damaged by the pipeline. Invariably, people saw themselves in the individuals in those stories—most famously Randy Thompson, a farmer and stockman from rural Nebraska whose land was in the path of the proposed pipeline. Before long, the campaign caught fire, growing from a small group of local liberal activists to a national coalition of farmers and ranchers, Native tribes, environmental activists, families, church leaders, and celebrities from across the political spectrum, all pledging to "Stand With Randy." Some joined based on their objection to the violation of personal property rights. Others were motivated to protect the treasured Ogallala Aquifer. Still others urged the powers-that-be to focus on building an energy infrastructure that benefited Americans, rather than greenlighting a massive export pipeline across the country to move Canadian oil to China. As of 2021, the pipeline's future remains in doubt, reeling from legal setbacks, disapproval from the Biden administration, and declining public favor. The civic power of the many trumped the well-financed and well-connected few.

It's important to note that the Keystone XL drama has unfolded over a decade and is, in fact, still unfolding. And it is but one cause of many. So remember that *civic power requires persistence and patience*. Wielding civic power for long-term, structural change entails a determination that often runs counter to our modern culture of instant gratification. Not to mention our time-honored political and governing structures, in slicing up power among federal, state, and local boards and bodies. Sustaining civic power becomes even more difficult when considering at each of the federal, state, and local levels, power is further separated among different branches of government, and then granularized across an array of departments, boards, commissions, and agencies. This can threaten to sap the energy of any cause or campaign, no matter how urgent or righteous—even those individuals and groups skilled in organizing, building, and exercising civic power struggle with this shape of things.

Which brings us back to the first step. In these moments, we can ask ourselves: *How can this be different? What must happen in order to create positive change?* Achieving true civic power means more than winning a few one-off battles. Creating meaningful, sustainable change means constantly re-imagining and, if necessary, restructuring our systems—governmental and otherwise. That way, the connections, stories, and activism of civic power can ensure the central functions and goals of those systems are centered on citizen engagement, involvement, and mutual accountability.

When people organize and systemize the use of civic power, the barriers that maintain the status quo are much more difficult to justify. Fortunately, democracy is flexible and adaptable. It thrives on new ideas, energy, and innovation. And it is unquestionably strengthened through the very existence of civic power.

—STEVE SMITH

12

Be a Citizen, Not a Consumer

Our democracy is not a business. It is not transactional.
It is built on mutual trust and action that require
much more than our narrow self-interests.

"YOU KNOW, WE SHOULD RUN THE GOVERNMENT LIKE
A BUSINESS." If you've ever found yourself in a discussion
about the state of American affairs, you've almost certainly
heard this notion at some point. This idea tends to come
from a well-intentioned place; often, it's offered as a remedy
for what might seem to be an oversized and inefficient government bureaucracy. Applying some good old-fashioned
business acumen to public affairs can sound attractive: Ask
10 Americans if they favor a higher grade of administrative
excellence and accountability in government, and 11 will
say yes.

The notion also tends to gain traction in times when
satisfaction with government is on the decline. One of its
first notable advocates was Woodrow Wilson when he was
a professor of political economy at Princeton. In 1887, sitting
snugly amid the Gilded Age, the future president posited
that certain administrative and management principles were

unchangeable and universal, regardless of their context. Public sector, private sector—it didn't matter. *Run government like a business.* Later researchers, observing the vast differences in the ways that such principles had to be applied between the private and public entities, largely discredited Wilson's theories. By that point, however, the notion had taken firm hold.

It should go without saying that government is not a business. Its purpose, priorities, and methods—protecting rights, upholding the rule of law, keeping citizens safe, and providing public services—differ greatly from that of business (profits, shareholders' interests, creating more customers). Still, Americans seem to learn and relearn this lesson through the ages. Sure, the two sectors intersect at a few key points. But their fundamental disjunction is proof that often, what is popular in theory doesn't pan out in the real world.

This book is about democracy, not economics. But we bring it up here because no matter the argument to strengthen our democratic society, our free-market, capitalistic economy is always a factor. It's always looming in the background and, often, it's right up front. This helps explain the staying power of *You know, we should run the government like a business*, and more importantly, it highlights one of its most persistent side effects: The idea that if the country is a business, then we must be its customers.

This is a dangerous mindset. "Consumer sovereignty"—the idea that the customer always knows best, that everyone should act in their own self-interests, and that ultimately, patriotism is measured by spending—puts our individual ledgers out of balance. That is, in our democratic republic, a citizen must not only have the right to *be*, but also carry the responsibility to *do*. And this can't be done only by consuming goods and services.

We recognize this is not easy in today's world, especially when considering that the forces of marketing and competitive politics have coalesced into an ever-encroaching daily influence in our lives. This omnipresent force dominates our very concept of the country, not to mention our individual places in it. Political parties and candidates, with terabytes of market research at their disposal, bombard us with increasingly granular, polished messages delivered by sophisticated algorithms. News media, once comfortable as loss leaders, now present their journalism as content for profit, and consider viewers "news consumers." It's no wonder, then, that we increasingly expect our candidates to be precisely tailored to fit our every personal opinion and taste, as if built *a la carte* for us in every conceivable way. After all, we are the customers. This is what we demand.

Yet, "democracy is not a synonym for the marketplace," political theorist Benjamin Barber once wrote. "Consumers speak the divisive rhetoric of *me*. Citizens invent the common language of *we*." Active and informed citizenship is necessary to fill the vacuum that consumerism leaves in our public sphere. Otherwise, it will be filled by all kinds of other forces positioning themselves for control over our society.

To strengthen our democracy, we must first strengthen the citizen side of our individual ledgers. That requires the recognition that our world is networked, interrelated, and interdependent. It requires the understanding that our democracy—just like our economy—is a complex, adaptive system in which all acts, large and small, accrue. And it requires us to acknowledge that mutual trust and confidence in one another, not dollars, is our most powerful currency.

By focusing beyond narrow self-interests and considering how our greater society can benefit, we can claim and wield incredible civic power. We can serve as a check on corporations from having undue influence in how we structure our society, and at the same time we can contribute to more effective—and fair—governance.

That's citizenship, not consumerism. In a nation where we have so many choices and are inundated by marketing, civic responsibility might seem counter-cultural. But it's an absolutely vital part of our shared democratic process. Without it, we lose our agency. We lose our seats at the table.

—STEVE SMITH

13

Focus Your Time, Talent & Treasure

Ordinary people participating out loud in democracy
builds broad civic strength. Find organizations and
movements that provide opportunities for us to
do things together that we could not do alone.

SO FAR, WE'VE USED the word *democracy* quite a bit. It may
give you pause. You may be asking: *Aren't we a Republic?*
There's a difference, isn't there? The answers are yes and no.
We define democracy not solely as systemic, with a narrow
focus on the forms and functions of our government. In
practice, we know that democracy must be more substantive, expansive and vigilant in times and places beyond the
Legislature and when it is in session.

Self-government goes beyond elections. When he traveled
across America in the mid-19th century, Alexis de Tocqueville noted that our democracy drew great power from the
extraordinary number of Americans who were volunteers,
advocates, and, quite simply, joiners. Whether it be participation in civic organizations, churches, political parties, or
associations, de Tocqueville noted, the resiliency of American democracy was found in our relentless *habit* of prac-

ticing it. We continue that tradition today: Our voluntary connections continue to develop civic skills and routines. Through them, we identify issues, share responsibility, build mutual goals, collaborate, and remain community-minded. Then we pass this down to our children and grandchildren, and the virtuous cycle continues.

These activities are often underrated ingredients in the recipe of American democracy. They are vital for a truly modern and robust democracy, because they bind us together and improve the *civic health* of our communities. When we are more connected to one another and to institutions, we are better positioned to solve local problems. The National Conference on Citizenship, a Washington, D.C.-based organization with which Civic Nebraska partners, defines *civic health* as the way that communities are organized to define and address public problems. Decades of data collected by the organization indicate that communities with strong civic health have higher employment rates, stronger schools, better physical health, and more responsive governments.

Not coincidentally, civically healthy communities also offer a wide range of ways citizens can reach beyond their private lives and come together to tackle common tasks. The reason can vary: We may be passionate about an issue; we may want to provide care for those in our communities; or we may feel a call to serve or practice a more intentional kind of citizenship. All are entry points to a more inclusive and loving society. Towns and cities with strong nonprofits, clubs, associations, and social movements empower their members to build and express collective interest and energy. It's also good for us as individuals. Civic activity, membership in civic organizations, and volunteering can contribute to healthier people both mentally and physically. This makes sense: Humans are social creatures. We long for connection, substance, and meaning. When we are civically active, we connect with others and make change in our communities. We check off all the boxes.

Some of us, thanks to accidents of birth, good luck, or achievement, are in a better position to act than others. Some of us enjoy advantages and privilege from our upbringing, education, and income. In these cases, it must be our *duty* to focus our time, talent, and treasure on joining other agents of democracy—organizations, associations, and movements— that activate a community's popular hopes and desires.

With every neighborhood clean-up, we say out loud that taking responsibility for our environment is necessary for everyone in our community's health, safety, and fortune.

Every time we volunteer at a local school, we help build the next generation of active, educated, critically thinking Americans.

With every donation—whether it be clothes, food, money, or our very blood—we literally give of ourselves for the benefit of our fellow Americans.

When we support groups and organizations that work to improve the quality of life for others, we invest in our community's long-term civic health.

When we hold voter registration drives, march, or protest, we build relationships, trust, and civic power that sustains our democracy.

We don't have to be nonstop activists 24 hours a day, seven days a week, 365 days a year. But if each of us resolves to step out of our private worlds and focus on the good of others, it can be both our duty and our joy to tend to our nation. And we will pass along a stronger, more vibrant democracy for future generations.

—STEVE SMITH

14

Raise All Voices

We have a democratic duty to lift up the voices
and share the stories of others, particularly those
of us who have been historically silenced.

THERE IS A BLACK-AND-WHITE vinyl sticker affixed to
the back of Gabriella Parsons' laptop computer that reads
Somebody Should Do Something. With that same laptop, she
takes her sticker's advice. The visual storyteller from Lincoln documents the lives of historically underrepresented
Nebraskans with an eye on creating systemic change. In 2018,
while partnering with the community-organizing partner-
ship Collective Impact Lincoln, Gabriella (or Gab as she
is best known) created *Stories of Impact*, a series of photos
and videos highlighting everyday residents of the city's low-
est-income neighborhoods. In 2020, she brought urgency
and humanity to the swelling eviction crisis with *Behind
on Rent*, a short film featuring Nebraskans facing the loss
of their homes. All the while, Gab coordinates the program
Untold Migrant Stories, which empowers young immigrants
to tell and share their stories through digital media.

It's tempting to offer up the cliché that Gab "gives voice to the voiceless." Through potent documentary storytelling, she certainly does leverage the modern communications methods at her disposal to lift up the stories of the underrepresented, the disadvantaged, and the vulnerable. But Gab also understands that "giving voice to the voiceless" is only half of the equation; the other half is ensuring that those voices are meaningfully *heard*.

That's why her work is fashioned to be more than just consumed; it's intended to start a conversation, to engage a broader community, and to inspire action. *Stories of Impact* led to public screenings and exhibition-style gatherings, including an event at a local Asian culture center that drew hundreds to a community discussion about broad community investment in lower-income neighborhoods. And with *Behind on Rent*, Gab took advantage of Zoom to host a virtual screening and roundtable discussion about housing issues that were exacerbated by coronavirus. Nearly 200 elected leaders, nonprofit heads, organizers, and community advocates participated.

Truly representative democracy happens when all voices, taken together, are heard. And that can only happen if all of us, regardless of station or background, have the capacity to tell our stories and express ourselves. Having a greater voice leads to more influence, a real ability to hold our officials and institutions accountable, the power to guide more inclusive priorities, and build a consensus around tackling the big issues of the day. Adding as many voices as possible to the existing debate opens the opportunity for new realities and new possibilities.

The good news is that right now, it's easier than ever to express ourselves to ever-larger audiences. Thanks to modern communications technology, projecting our voices in ways that were unimaginable 25 years ago is practically second nature. Groups that once struggled to establish a foothold in the national conversation now can raise their visibility with a click of a mouse, a mass email, or a text. From the Tea Party to Black Lives Matter, like-minded Americans quickly and effectively connect across time and space. And they are demanding their say.

Wouldn't it be wonderful if this is where the story ends? The democratization of information systems creates true equality. But as we know, this process does not exist in a vacuum. Asymmetrical structures of power still sustain the status quo, and they have proven to be quite sturdy. Even as more people find new ways to advance their views through mobile technology and social networking, those at the top use the same tools to maintain the retrenchment, social exclusion, and marginalization that first propelled them to power. And, of course, our nation's political dynamics fortify this framework, with powerful interests creating their own "bubbles" to insulate themselves from the wants and needs of ordinary Americans. In such a fragmented and noisy environment, does a temporarily trending hashtag or a viral video really make a bit of difference?

It would be easy to say no. When the loudest and most powerful voices threaten to drown out all others, those who remain unheard can become isolated, depressed, or even angry. Over time, this threatens to erode our collective civic health. Left untended, it fuels distrust, belligerence, broken relationships, and a civil society too worn down to function. Trapped in our singular worldviews, we become increasingly polarized and quick to conflict. And nothing changes.

And yet, a world overwhelmed by sound and fury can be tamed by the oldest of human currencies: our stories. It can be brought to heel by the basic law that The Many are greater than The Few. As the example of Bold Nebraska showed, our stories have immense power. They elicit emotions, humanize abstract concepts, build deeper connections to the world around us, and bring purpose to our discourse. As democratic citizens, it is our obligation to amplify others' voices and stories in the pursuit of a more equal society. Being careful not to *be* those voices, we can take substantive steps toward transforming communities and reforming institutions into places and structures where all voices are respected and valued.

This has lasting, positive effects on democracy—and on us as individuals. Being open to someone else's perspective is emotionally and psychologically healthy. And, research shows, so is *providing* our perspective to another person or group of people. This makes perfect sense: All humans desire to be heard and understood; when our words and experiences are acknowledged, we feel respected and trusted. Respect and trust are also infectious. They lead to cooperation, consensus, and mutual concern.

In person or online, via word of mouth or in our social networks, whether we are a talented documentary filmmaker or whether we merely hit "Share," we must never stop raising others' voices. We must never stop spreading the stories of others. Word by word, frame by frame, more and more people will go from unheard to heard, misunderstood to understood. From there, anything is possible.

—STEVE SMITH

Conversation Starters: Empowerment

* Do you volunteer your time for local organizations? Why?

* Who are your community's formal and informal leaders?

* Where can people of different backgrounds go to connect?

* Does your community support entrepreneurship?

* Is your community welcoming? Do new people want to move there? Why or why not?

* What's more important, being an individual or part of a community?

PART FOUR

Choose Optimism

Embrace new ideas and put them into action. Learn together today to implement change tomorrow.

15

Envision a More Perfect Union

If you can imagine what a safe, prosperous, and healthy
America for all looks like, then it is achievable.

IN 1971, TWO DAYS AFTER HIS THIRTY-FIRST BIRTHDAY,
John Lennon released what would become one of the most
well-known and influential songs in music history. The song,
"Imagine," asked us to simply picture a better world—"it's
easy if you try." Though it was written off as utopian non-
sense in some corners (the notorious biographer Albert
Goldman called it "a hippie wishing well full of pennyweight
dreams"), it remains an influential anthem of idealism today.

You may be asking: What does a starry-eyed song from
the Vietnam era have to do with strengthening modern
democracy? Plenty. The first and most important step in
taking meaningful action requires much more than simply
wishing things will get better. Breaking loose from such static
citizenship starts with actively conceptualizing a better way
forward. If we dare to imagine what a safe, prosperous, and
healthy America for all looks like, we have taken the first
step toward making that America a reality.

This necessitates a measure of optimism and curiosity. Looking around at the way things are, picturing a better way, and then asking *Why not?* requires tamping down the knee-jerk pessimism that has become all too familiar when we consider our individual impact in modern society. Too often, we're led to believe that what we think doesn't matter; that no matter what, nothing can change. Or, if it does, it's only in small ways and around the edges.

History, meantime, suggests that the disillusioned and the disaffected do not readily participate in a system that they believe has failed them. Yet, we've seen evidence to the contrary time and again in America. The record number of voters in November reminds us that our confidence in democracy is an old and powerful American trait. It has driven us forward, ever since overtaxed British subjects first considered what a free, independent America might look like. This devotion is woven through our American story, from enslaved peoples breaking free, to exploited workers banding together and finding strength in numbers, to women reaching for the ballot at long last. This faith helped extinguish Jim Crow, lift millions out of poverty, end unjust wars, and inspire millions more to claim their American rights. From Philadelphia to Seneca Falls to Selma to Stonewall, faith grew into ideas, ideas grew into connections, and connections grew into powerful and historic movements. The rest is, quite literally, history.

A clear lesson from the last decade is that democracy does not run on autopilot. It does not travel in a straight line.

Absent a clear vision of a more perfect union (and with leaders unwilling or unable to put that vision into action), our democracy can stray from these progressive values. Our civil society, beaten down but not beaten, has served as a backstop against the backslide. But in the long term, civil society requires more than a sense of duty or requirement to stand up in times of crisis. When we act, every day, for reasons beyond money or because we are compelled by law—if we act because we are motivated by the idea of something bigger—we advance democracy. We begin to move forward again.

We can look to Washington, D.C., or to the Statehouse, or to City Hall to handle this for us. But there have been far too many examples of poor governance, intellectually or morally absent leadership, and repugnant conduct from those elected to represent us. We can assume, then, that this is how we citizens should act, as well. Too often, our discourse devolves to disagreements over who is the bigger hypocrite, and is absent any vision or aspiration of the type of community, state, or nation we wish to be. But this is not a reason to pack it in and call it quits.

This is a time for us all to step into the yawning space that many of our leaders have left vacant. In fact, it is already happening. From organizations and individuals of all ages who provide support for fellow-citizens, to those who are conceiving policies, outlining plans, and taking meaningful action, our communities are changing, growing, and progressing right now.

Such optimism runs counter to the long history of humanity. The assumption that things eventually get better isn't how civilizations have functioned over the millennia; the communal concepts of development, growth, and advancement reach back only to the European Enlightenment, a blink of an eye in human history. For thousands of years before that, most societies assumed that any achievements made during the good times were fleeting, and that eras of peace and harmony were already behind them. This is a powerful legacy to overcome. Even the modern American mindset cannot fully escape it. Our country has never advanced neatly, in an orderly or even peaceful fashion. Our history is full of people rushing forward to claim their rightful power, hitting walls of opposition, and then finding ways around those walls. Along the way, Americans have stretched the imaginations and the intent of our Founders—those wild-eyed dreamers of their day—by expanding the blessings of liberty to those of every race, gender, background, and creed. We know a more perfect union is possible because we've been party to that perfection.

Let's keep our imagination at the center of our citizenship. Then, when we activate in support of our ideals, we inspire others to center their citizenship alongside ours. That's how movements spread. That's how they take on new shapes, new character, and new advocates, and eventually realize the change they seek. Every great achievement started by picturing how something—or *everything*—might be different.

Imagine that. It's easy if you try.

—STEVE SMITH

16

Spread the Faith

> Democracy works because we believe in it—that
> it is worth sustaining and advancing. If we lose
> faith in that notion, our institutions and systems
> disintegrate. Then, we lose everything.

EARLIER WE REFLECTED ON the January 2021 assault on the U.S. Capitol. Our point was that democracy depends on the truth; that without the acceptance of shared facts, democracy ceases to be. Now, if you'll indulge us, we'd like you to join us on the other end of the spectrum. Let's apply that same urgency to the need for faith.

Not the religious kind, necessarily, but faith in our democracy. In its systems, processes, people, institutions, and its future. Facts and faith are not mutually exclusive: Nearly everything we do has some faith to it, from planting a garden in the spring to scheduling an outdoor wedding to wearing our favorite team's colors though they might be three-touchdown underdogs.

The same is true with democracy.

Eric Liu, the founder of Seattle-based Citizen University, which works to build a spirit of powerful citizenship among

Americans, is fond of saying *democracy works only if enough people believe democracy works*. In recent years, amid unprecedented tumult, it's understandable to wonder if this is the case anymore. The images of the Capitol insurrection were eye-opening in so many ways, but most of all, they told us this: Those who participated have lost their faith in democracy. And if polls are to be believed, many who weren't at the Capitol have, as well: Months after President Biden took office, reliable surveys showed vast numbers of those who voted for former President Trump still believed that their candidate was cheated out of a second term. By accepting a false rigged-election narrative despite overwhelming evidence to the contrary, they have put the baseless opinions of one man above their faith in America.

Can these Americans be brought back to a safe place, where they can muster a modicum of trust in our American institutions? We certainly hope so. Ultimately, it is their choice and their choice alone. But it is important that the rest of us—*and that's most of us*—keep the faith, show our faith, and spread our faith. Faith in our systems, in our institutions, and in one another. This can only help make the path for our fellow-citizens' safe return a little more likely, and slightly easier.

We do this knowing that, yes, QAnon and "alternate facts" are contagious. But so is democracy. In fact, if we had to place a bet, we'd bet the house on democracy. Throughout our history, it has been the dominant contagion. It might not always feel like it as we trudge through our American experiment, day by day and struggle by struggle, but taking the long view, democracy enjoys an excellent track record.

We have painted with a broad brush. The work of democracy requires persistence in the face of missteps and false starts, of which there will be many. From the Founding, change and progress has been the story of America. History calls on us, in this pivotal decade, to summon our trust in America once more. In the 2020s, we can harness the rejuvenating power of faith for the struggle ahead. So let's keep asking those age-old questions that have moved mountains throughout our American story: *How can things be different? How can things be better? How can WE be better?* And then, when we find the answers, let's go to work. Let's make it reality.

Be optimistic. Spread confidence in our systems, our institutions, and our democratic future. Because democracy is contagious. *It has worked because enough people have believed it works.* And so it must continue to be. Inevitably, there will be difficult days for our country. During these times, it always will be tempting to wallow in the dark, to contemplate whether we are truly progressing. But, to paraphrase John Lewis, the work is not the struggle of a day. It's not the struggle of a week, a month, or a year. It is of a lifetime.

And that? That requires faith.

— STEVE SMITH

17

Be Patriotic

Loving our country requires perseverance
and devotion to our founding creed of
liberty and equality—and more.

CLOSE YOUR EYES AND PICTURE A PATRIOT. What comes
to you? Maybe your mind's eye reflexively summons those
who fought for the cause of liberty: a Minuteman halting
the British at the Old North Bridge; a Union soldier holding
the line at Gettysburg; Marines lifting Old Glory on a craggy
Pacific island. Or maybe you conjure other varieties of freedom fighters: conductors on the Underground Railroad;
Freedom Riders busing along perilous Southern roadways;
a King whose dream still resonates across our land. Reflecting further, maybe you see presidents lifting up the nation
during crisis; triumphant athletes in red, white, and blue;
motorcyclists flanking grieving military families; protestors
on the public square; or even, simply, a neighbor lowering
and folding her front-porch flag at sundown.

Each of these images is as valid as the next. Each con-
veys a distinct contour of patriotism, popular or otherwise, that is ingrained in our American consciousness. It's

appropriate, too, that our descriptions and definitions of American patriotism are robust, plentiful as well as diverse: Compared with the rest of the world, we Americans spend lots of time thinking about and debating what is patriotic. The World Values Survey, for instance, always finds that Americans are at or near the top in expressing pride in our nationality.

It might be surprising to hear, then, that polls taken at the same time have consistently found that patriotism is on the decline in the United States. An annual Gallup survey on the topic, for instance, found 70 percent of us were "extremely proud" to be Americans in 2003. By 2019, the number had skidded to a mere 47 percent.

Perhaps some of the decline is due to our increasingly polarized politics. In a time of extreme partisanship, it's almost reflexive to conflate the country with its leaders, for good or for bad. An American whose patriotism is contingent on whether their party is in power, though, is a *partisan*, not a patriot. Second, as we are well aware, patriotism can be twisted to fit all sorts of partisan frames—but, as we also are well aware, obedience to an ideology or its actors is not the same as loving our country. Third, part of the decline is certainly from some citizens' reticence to embrace the overt, populist brand of star-spangled adulation, a love-it-or-leave-it fervor that forces one on one side of an arbitrary, yet very bright line. And finally, some point to the cosmopolitan nature of our increasingly interconnected world as proof that national loyalty is steadily becoming obsolete.

It must not. Patriotism, regardless of our politics, is an indispensable ingredient that strengthens our social bonds, solidifies our mutuality, and shapes our common purpose. Patriotism is absolutely necessary as we carry our democratic experiment forward. It also is not simple: Unlike most other nations, which forge their origins and ethos in a common language, culture, and ethnicity, the United States was created from a moral ideal. Naturally, then, this is the most durable strand of our patriotism—*America-as-idea*. This aspirational patriotism drives us, unceasingly, toward that often-mentioned, never-attained "more perfect union." *America-as-idea* flows immaculately from our national spirit: the United States, and her people, champion liberty and justice for all, above all.

This is remarkable, especially since in the course of more than two centuries our country has gone from 13 eastern states to a continent-spanning 50 (plus territories). History is full of nations that were irreparably damaged by expansion, ambition, and growth. Yet equality and democracy have *not* become more abstract in America as we have advanced. Our founding principles persist. They still form the core of our patriotism.

Yet, we know there has to be more. It can't just be a set of intangibles, can it? That is why we also find patriotism in other ways. We find it in our singular traditions. We find it our distinct (and also unwieldy) culture. We find it in the very spaces across this continent on which we live. And, above all, we find it in our shared story: In the nearly 250 years since the Revolution, we have assembled a historical account to complement and challenge the abstract values given to us by the Founders. We've all been shaped by this history: the sacrifices of war; the shame of slavery; the suffering of the Great Depression; the triumph of modern innovation; the daring that took us to the moon. This story is fundamental to our American identity. It is *America-as-foundation*. It matters. With such racially, ethnically, and geographically diverse citizens, these two concepts of patriotism can be unanimous in many ways and at the same time fragmented by region, station, and culture. It can be both local and national. It can stretch across time and space and continue to blend our modern culture with our founding creed.

Through it all, American patriotism can be incredibly hard to define, which is probably why we spend so much time talking about it. But this much is clear: An America that swings wildly between a puffed-up vision of an infallible, righteous power at one extreme to an ill-natured, self-loathing union at the other is not an America that is long for this world.

Our patriotism, at its best, is both aspirational and inspirational, inclusive and exceptional. American patriotism—a clear-headed, sincere patriotism—reckons with and reflects on our national ideals and foundations. It is an acknowledgment that America is an imperfect, yet consequential nation. And it tells us that, as patriots, it is our responsibility to sustain it.

—STEVE SMITH

18

Show Up

> Apathy is democracy's mortal foe. Ask yourself
> what you are prepared to do, out in the open,
> to defend and protect democratic ideals.

"DEMOCRACY IS NOT A SPECTATOR SPORT." That's a popular saying among activists and advocates, regardless of where they are on the political spectrum. In other words, we get out of democracy what we put into it. If we sit back and rely on others' time, talent, and treasure to shape our shared society, we surrender our ability to co-create our shared democratic reality. But by stepping into the public square, by joining other active and engaged citizens, we forge bonds and continually connect with one another in pursuit of substantive change. Through these contacts, we become advocates in creating, constructing, and protecting our civic society. So, it's probably more accurate to add a line to that popular saying: *Democracy is not a spectator sport, it's a contact sport.*

As Americans, we have a tradition of activating and advocating for our beliefs. This has taken many forms, from sit-ins and boycotts to marches and vigils, from speeches to public art and performances. These traditions are enshrined in our founding doctrine, which bestows upon us the rights and responsibilities to participate with purpose—out in the open—and inspire others to join in. Public activism is a time-honored building block of America.

These democratic activities charge us with civic power. They confirm to us that others in our community see the world as we do. And by speaking our truths and bearing witness, we contribute to a sense of being part of something that is larger than ourselves. Collective action is a powerful bonding agent; our public participation in movements, marches, and organized dissent sustains long-term momentum for our chosen cause. It transforms us from casual participants to lifelong activists.

These pursuits have more urgent purposes, of course. At their core, they are a straightforward demand for change. They're a loud cry for a wider understanding of an issue, a call to right a wrong or a series of wrongs. They don't only draw power from their numbers, but from urgency. Someone just learning of the issue at hand for the first time may see a protest, march, or performance and ask: *What prompted so many people to show up, and why today?* Demonstrations that convey the issue at hand is so urgent that the time for idleness is over often lead to larger conversations, which can then lead to lasting and meaningful change.

You might be thinking: *I thought that was what voting was for.* You'll get no argument here about the importance of casting ballots as a direct and potent way to affect change.

Voting, as we'll see in the next section, is absolutely fundamental to democracy. It's also a natural progression from being a casual participant to engaged activist to lifelong voter. While protests tend to emerge when Americans feel their voices are not being heard and urgency demands we cannot wait for the next Election Day, channeling street-level activism into electoral power is a key step to breakthrough change. Steadily and surely, social movements change the status quo.

"Power concedes nothing without a demand," Frederick Douglass once said. Recent movements have confirmed the resonant truth of Douglass's words—the fight for racial justice, for science and for religious freedom, for women's empowerment, for gun rights and gun reform all have displayed that democracy is a contact sport. That very fact means we can't leave it to others to show up for us.

—STEVE SMITH

19

Fight for Voting Rights

Without the right to vote, there is no method to
hold our leaders accountable and no real way for our
values and vision to be represented in our institutions.
This most basic right is never guaranteed. It must be
championed, defended, and exercised to the fullest.

VOTING IS OUR MOST CHERISHED AMERICAN RIGHT.
Unfortunately, in some corners, the very idea that it is a right
at all is still up for debate. There are those in the political
and legal worlds who maintain voting is a privilege, something to be earned once a citizen is deemed truly worthy of
the franchise. To justify this view, proponents point to the
language of the U.S. Constitution: Nowhere in our founding
document, they often say, is it guaranteed that all people
have the right to vote.

Here's the flaw in that assessment: If an affirmative guar-
antee is the standard for rights as spelled out by our Constitution, then there are very few rights actually enshrined in
it. It's just not how our Constitution is written. In fact, the
Bill of Rights was written purposely so that it limited *government*, not *individuals*. You see this most clearly in phrases

throughout the first ten amendments such as "Congress shall make no law . . ." and ". . . shall not be abridged."

As our nation progressed from independence to expansion to secession to Civil War to Reconstruction, the right to vote became more and more explicit in the Constitution. Starting with the Fourteenth and Fifteenth amendments, which paved the way for equality under the law and prohibited the exclusion of non-white men and freed male slaves from the franchise, the phrase "right to vote" has appeared repeatedly in the Constitution.

And almost immediately after the phrase was written down, so too were restrictions on these rights. Such strictures strike at the heart of a representative government. As anyone with a cursory understanding of the long fight for voting rights knows, our nation has made steady but uneven progress in this realm. While we have obviously invited more Americans into the democratic fold throughout our history, we also have experienced clear periods of backsliding, when voter suppression and disenfranchisement dominated. Simply put, the ability to vote—and, therefore, the right to vote—has not always been within reach for all Americans. From African Americans and Natives, to women of all races and ethnicities, the fight has been for that most fundamental of democratic rights: a seat at the table and the ability for their voices to be heard.

We continue this fight today.

While we would like to view the history of voting rights as one glorious march to universal suffrage, the fact of the matter is that progress ebbs and flows, and even retreats. Yes, federal involvement in voting rights has increased over time, but significant portions of election law still remain out of federal reach. The right to vote that is mentioned in later amendments of the Constitution prohibits different forms of legal discrimination, leaving many voting-related matters at the discretion of individual states.

For example, in most U.S. states, residents must register well before the date of an election to vote in it, and states offer different methods of registration. Others may require voters to present official government identification at their polling place before they are allowed to vote. Still other states continue to disenfranchise those who have paid their debts to society—Nebraska, for example, requires an arbitrary two-year waiting period on top of the full completion of a sentence before ex-felons are even *eligible* to vote. In 2021, Nebraska's rules remained among the most restrictive in the nation in this area.

Only time will tell how recent history and the present day will be remembered regarding our commitment to basic American ideals. For decades, the protections of the 1965 Voting Rights Act served as bulwarks against the suppression schemes that were staples across the Old Confederacy: poll taxes, literacy tests, and a litany of other bureaucratic restrictions that denied millions their rightful access to the ballot. But the landmark 2013 *Shelby County v. Holder* ruling, which gutted key provisions of the Voting Rights Act, ushered in a new era of voter suppression. By 2018, nearly

1,000 polling places had been closed across the country, many in predominantly African American areas. Images of lines of voters stretching down the block have become commonplace on Election Day. Combined with dozens of states imposing strict voter ID laws that disproportionately affect minorities, the poor, and the elderly; cutting early-voting periods to make it harder for more people to vote; and conducting aggressive voter purges of those who allegedly are ineligible, what was true before 1965 remains true today: For many Americans, the right to vote is *never* guaranteed.

This is why it must be exercised, championed, and defended to its fullest. Always.

We must start by voting in every single election—federal, state, and local, no exceptions. This is *quite literally* the least we can do as Americans. The good news is that it not only fulfills our basic responsibility as citizens, but if enough people do it, it also builds civic power in our community. It is a sober truth of modern politics that communities with higher voting rates receive more attention and investment from elected officials. If we and our neighbors choose to not exercise our voting power, we surrender it to others. In an ideal society, we might be able to fully trust our fellow-citizens to advocate for our particular well-being. But in reality, surrendering our vote allows those with their, not our, interests in mind to decide our future.

Simply voting is not enough, however. By championing our very right to vote, we stand as examples to others in the exercise of civic power. Whether it is placing a sign for a candidate or an issue in our yards or apartment windows, affixing a campaign bumper sticker on our vehicles, or visibly spending our social capital on being politically active and casting our ballots, we strengthen the right to vote for ourselves and, importantly, for others.

Finally, by advocating for ourselves and all voters—whether by testifying on behalf of legislation that makes voting or registering to vote easier, or by writing letters to the editor opposing harmful proposals such as voter ID or restrictions on voting by mail—we actively defend the right to vote.

Our right to vote is aspirational, with the power to create meaningful change. It is a necessary one that holds our leaders to account. And it is an active one that builds our values and dreams into our institutions, the right upon which all other rights are possible. As Americans, voting is our birthright. But it is no privilege. Fight for it.

—STEVE SMITH

20

Balance Hope & Conviction

*Don't despair. Reaching a shared vision will
take time, toil, and effort. Together, these forces
of progress move us to a better place.*

IN THE WORLD OF DESIGN, THERE IS A CONCEPT known
as *asymmetrical balance*. It's the idea that you can find balance without symmetry or equilibrium; that oddities or irregularities can create beauty. People often wonder if it isn't a similar asymmetrical balance that has allowed us to create progress within our own systems and, writ large, society. We don't seek change for the sake of change but because the scale feels tipped—because of unsolved issues, inequalities, and unmet needs. Because there is a hunger for better. There is a need to feel balance.

To reach for better and to create that balance, we need to be able to sustain both conviction and hope. Conviction presses us forward. Hope provides us the space to listen and understand that, if we don't all start at the same place, getting to the end of a shared vision will take time and understanding. Together, these two ideals tell us that while we are not there yet, we will be.

To collectively sustain these two essential factors, we must create a pace and cadence that allows the system to find a sense of security in the urgency to find a solution. Sometimes that means we have to be comfortable sitting in the smaller successes along the way, giving time to allow others to feel comfortable moving forward. It's the creation of hope, without losing sight of the ultimate goal. That's balance without symmetry.

And after a time of slowing down, conviction tells us it's time to work on the next step and to draw closer to the ultimate goal. To grab the understanding and support of later adapters and to figure out what the next small success looks like.

Without hope, we will never take the first meaningful step forward. And without conviction, we will settle for a lesser compromise. It takes both, sometimes in complete balance and sometimes in asymmetrical balance, but always with one on each side of the scale.

Often, to ensure we have both these items embedded in the system's culture, it takes a key person or group of people. Let's call them *grassroots champions*—someone to be willing to ask important questions, to tell the story in a way that creates shared buy-in, and to develop for everyone a clearer picture of what "better" looks like. Grassroots champions are experts in understanding the nuts and bolts of what is needed for the system to run well. They also know who has the right amount of both hope and conviction for the end to be a part of creating change. They engage those people in a meaningful way that matches their strengths and interests. Grassroots champions also create and hold the space needed to allow healthy conflict and manage the balance of conviction against hope so that the dynamic stays both positive and progressive.

To do this long term, it takes a foundation of trust. It also takes a system of broad support to usher those champions through the most divisive times, to keep them settled in the simmer of the slow successes. Through this relationship, the champion facilitates the environment needed for change and the system must acknowledge and support the champions so they can persevere, encouraging us all to cling to hope and be sustained by conviction.

We need our champions to continue to put themselves out on the edge, to reach for the next step, and to ask us all to join along. While incredibly rewarding at times, it can also be a difficult and lonely position to be in. Two distinctive roles, both needed for success.

It can be a difficult process to create meaningful change that protects and expands our democracy. Conviction is fueled by passion and hope, by an innate belief in something *better*. But *better* is worth it. *Better* lifts us all. It doesn't leave one side behind or discount the values of others.

Progress may not always feel similar or alike or adequate, but it is movement in the right direction. It's the balance without symmetry as we move toward *better*. And after enough small nudges and successes worth celebrating, we find ourselves having run the long game, and balance the scales.

—MELISSA GARCIA

Conversation Starters: Optimism

* Do you feel that you are an important part of the political process?

* Do you believe our country's "best days" are still to come, or have they come and gone?

* What does it mean to you to be "politically active"?

* In what ways do you engage with or support your elected officials?

* Have you ever attended a protest or rally? Why or why not?

* How do you think youth can best be involved in our political process?

* What does America 20 years from now look like to you?

Resources

RESOURCES

TEXTS, SPEECHES AND DOCUMENTS

The Social Contract,
Jean Jacque Rousseau (1762)

The Declaration of
Independence,
Continental Congress (1776)

The Constitution of the United
States of America,
including all later amendments
(1789)

Federalist 51,
James Madison in 1788

On Liberty,
John Stuart Mill (1859)

Declaration of Sentiments,
Elizabeth Cady Stanton (1848)

"Ain't I a Woman,"
Sojourner Truth (1851)

Dred Scott's Appeal,
Chief Justice Roger Taney
(1857)

Lincoln-Douglas debates,
Abraham Lincoln and Stephen
A. Douglas (1858)

Letter from a Birmingham Jail,
Martin Luther King (1963)

The Gettysburg Address,
Abraham Lincoln (1863)

"I Have a Dream,"
Martin Luther King Jr. (1963)

Four Freedoms,
Franklin D. Roosevelt (1941)

Inaugural Address,
John F. Kennedy (1961)

Further Reading

1. CHOOSE COMMUNITY

The Art of Gathering: How We Meet and Why It Matters
Priya Parker (2018)

*Hope for Democracy: How Citizens Can
Bring Reason Back Into Politics*
John Gastil & Katherine R. Knobloch (2019)

On Democracy
Robert Dahl (2010)

2. CHOOSE LEARNING

Why Learn History (When It's Already on Your Phone)
Sam Wineburg (2018)

*The Righteous Mind: Why Good People are
Divided by Religion and Politics*
Jonathan Haidt (2012)

I Think You're Wrong (But I'm Listening)
Sarah Stewart Holland and Beth Silvers (2019)

3. CHOOSE EMPOWERMENT

*You're More Powerful Than You Think: A Citizen's
Guide to Making Change Happen*
Eric Liu (2017)

Engines of Liberty: How Citizen Movements Succeed
David Cole (2016)

The Givers: Wealth, Power and Philanthropy in a New Gilded Age
David Callahan (2017)

4. CHOOSE OPTIMISM

*The Upswing: How America Came Together a
Century Ago and How We Can Do It Again*
Robert Putnam and Shaylyn Romney Garrett (2020)

Civic Hope: How Ordinary Americans Keep Democracy Alive
Roderick P. Hart (2018)

Unrigged: How Americans are Battling Back to Save Democracy
David Daley (2020)

About Civic Nebraska

Founded in Lincoln in 2008, Civic Nebraska creates a more modern and robust democracy for all Nebraskans. Through youth civic leadership, civic health programs, and nonpartisan voting rights initiatives, Civic Nebraska builds a community in which Nebraskans of all ages and backgrounds join to take action to strengthen democracy in innovative and meaningful ways.

Learn more at CivicNebraska.org.